GRAPHIC BIOGRAPHIES

BENEDICT ARNOLD

AMERICAN HERO AND TRAITOR

by Michael Burgan
illustrated by Terry Beatty

Consultant:
Wayne K. Bodle, PhD
Department of History
Indiana University of Pennsylvania

Capstone
press

Mankato, Minnesota

Graphic Library is published by Capstone Press,
151 Good Counsel Drive, P.O. Box 669, Mankato, Minnesota 56002.
www.capstonepress.com

1 2 3 4 5 6 12 11 10 09 08 07

Library of Congress Cataloging-in-Publication Data
Burgan, Michael.
    Benedict Arnold : American hero and traitor / by Michael Burgan; illustrated by Terry Beatty.
    p. cm.—(Graphic library. Graphic biographies)
    Includes bibliographical references and index.
    ISBN-13: 978-0-7368-6854-9 (hardcover)
    ISBN-10: 0-7368-6854-2 (hardcover)
    ISBN-13: 978-0-7906-4 (softcover pbk.)
    ISBN-10: 0-7368-7906-4 (softcover pbk.)
    1. Arnold, Benedict, 1741–1801—Juvenile literature. 2. American loyalists—Biography—Juvenile
literature. 3. Generals—United States—Biography—Juvenile literature. 4. United States. Continental
Army—Biography—Juvenile literature. 5. United States—History—Revolution, 1775–1783—Juvenile
literature. 6. Graphic novels. I. Beatty, Terry, ill. II. Title. III. Series.
E278.A7B87 2007
973.3'82092—dc22   2006027985

Summary: In graphic novel format, tells the story of Benedict Arnold's heroism and betrayal during
    the American Revolution.

Designers
Alison Thiele and Thomas Emery

Production Designer
Kim Brown

Colorist
Scott Larson

Editor
Martha E. H. Rustad

Editor's note: Direct quotations from primary sources are indicated by a yellow background.

Direct quotations appear on the following pages:
Page 14, from a 1777 letter from Benedict Arnold to General George Washington, as published in
    The Life of Benedict Arnold: His Patriotism and His Treason by Isaac N. Arnold (Chicago:
    Jansen, McClurg, and Company, 1880).
Page 22, from the Public Papers of Sir Henry Clinton at the University of Michigan, Ann Arbor, as
    published in *The Man in the Mirror: A Life of Benedict Arnold* by Clare Brandt (New York:
    Random House, 1994).
Page 26, from an account of the battle at Fort Griswold by Thomas Hertell, as published in *The Battle
    of Groton Heights: A Collection of Narratives, Official Reports, Records, & c., of the Storming of
    Fort Griswold, and the Burning of New London by British Troops, Under the Command of
    Brig.-Gen. Benedict Arnold, on the Sixth of September, 1781* by William Wallace Harris
    (New London, 1870).

TABLE OF CONTENTS

CHAPTER 1

RISE OF A YOUNG PATRIOT

In 1754, 13-year-old Benedict Arnold attended a private school in Canterbury, Connecticut. For many years, his father had been a successful merchant in nearby Norwich. The family's good fortunes, however, came to an end.

Benedict, your parents can't afford your schooling anymore. You'll have to go home.

Arnold's mother, Hannah, wanted her son to learn a trade, since he could not afford to go to college.

I've talked to my cousins, the Lathrops. They'll take you on as an apprentice at their drug store.

I'll work hard, Mother. You'll be proud of me.

As an apprentice, Arnold worked for the Lathrops for several years. In return, they gave him a place to live and taught him their business.

With any luck, Benedict, you'll have your own store some day.

That's my plan, sir. I want to make as much money as I can. I'll show everyone that the Arnolds are successful.

In 1762, with help from the Lathrops, 21-year-old Arnold opened his own shop in New Haven, Connecticut.

Congratulations, Mr. Arnold! I hear your business is a success. But tell me, what is Sibi Totique?

B. Arnold Druggist
Book-seller, &c
From London
Sibi Totique

That's my motto. In Latin, it means "For himself and for all." I help myself by helping others.

CHAPTER 2
BATTLEFIELD HERO

In June 1775, the Continental Congress gave control of Fort Ticonderoga to Connecticut. Angry about losing his command, Arnold met with the commander of the Continental Army, General George Washington.

Some of our political leaders don't like you, Mr. Arnold. They say you always do things your own way. But I think you're an excellent commander.

Thank you, sir.

Do you have any ideas for what to do next?

We should invade Canada.

I agree.

The fighting continued until dark. Arnold considered what to do next.

British ships chased the Americans. Arnold fought three of them so that his other ships could escape.

We've lost several ships. The British are sure to attack again tomorrow. What should we do?

We'll sneak past the British in the fog. Place a lantern at the rear of each ship, for the next one to follow.

We never could have beaten the British on the water. But at least now they won't get us or our ship.

Arnold soon returned to Fort Ticonderoga.

We were lucky to escape. We lost too many men and ships. The mission failed.

Not at all, Arnold. The British returned to Canada. If not for you, they would have taken Ticonderoga. We'll keep control of the Hudson River—for now.

13

CHAPTER 3

FROM HERO TO TRAITOR

Arnold spent months recovering from his wound. In June 1778, he became the military commander of Philadelphia. British troops had just left the city. As commander, Arnold soon angered some residents.

How can General Arnold marry Margaret Shippen? Her father is loyal to the British.

And what about Arnold's business deals? He works with men who oppose patriots like us.

Joseph Reed was a patriot leader in Philadelphia.

General Arnold is corrupt and not worthy to serve here. He has broken the law, and we want Congress to take action.

18

19

23

CHAPTER 4

WITH THE BRITISH

Arnold was soon commanding loyalist troops fighting for the British. Whether he knew it or not, soldiers on both sides now hated him.

How can you trust someone who turns against his own country?

You know that officer who died the other day? I heard a rumor that Arnold poisoned him. And it's his fault we lost poor Major Andre.

In January 1781, Arnold fought for the British in Virginia. He then returned to New York with a plan.

General Clinton, the ships sailing from New London are hurting our fleet. Let me seize the city and put an end to that.

You do know the area better than us. All right, Arnold, take your men to Connecticut.

In September, Arnold led the raid on New London. This seaport on the Thames River was just 15 miles south of his hometown of Norwich. Arnold's men quickly took control of the city.

Destroy the ships and anything that can be used for war. But no looting.

One of the ships was filled with gunpowder. It exploded, starting a fire that spread to homes and shops in the city.

Across the river, fierce fighting went on at Fort Griswold. Finally, the Americans surrendered to Arnold's forces.

Who commands this fort?

Sir, I had that honor but now you have.

The loyalist commander stabbed the American officer as he tried to surrender. An American nearby then lunged forward with his sword. In seconds, the loyalists were attacking the Americans.

Kill them all! Kill all the rebels!

Arnold's New London raid was one of the most destructive of the entire war.

In October 1781, Washington's army defeated the British at a major battle in Yorktown, Virginia. Arnold had returned to New York.

We can still beat the rebels. Let me go to England. I must convince the king to let me lead a loyalist army.

BENEDICT ARNOLD

Benedict Arnold was born January 14, 1741, in Norwich, Connecticut. Arnold was the fifth person in his family with that name. The first Benedict Arnold served as governor of Rhode Island Colony during the 1660s and 1670s.

Arnold has sometimes been called the "Father of the American Navy" because of the fleet he built on Lake Champlain in 1776.

At his court-martial in 1779, Arnold argued he was innocent of the major charges against him. The court found that he did not break the law, but he had twice acted improperly. For his punishment, Arnold received a public scolding from General Washington.

After his arrest, Major John Andre was hanged as a spy. Andre had been a popular officer, and many British soldiers and citizens blamed Arnold for his death.

The U.S. Constitution is the document that outlines the form of government used in the United States. The only crime defined in the Constitution is treason. It is defined as a citizen waging war against the United States or aiding an enemy during wartime.

For turning over West Point, Arnold wanted the British to pay him a fee that would be equal to $1.6 million today. He eventually received less than half of that, though the British also paid him a salary every year for the rest of his life.

Some patriot soldiers angered by Arnold's treason hoped to kill or capture him in battle. Many claimed that they wanted to cut off the leg he wounded at Quebec and Saratoga. They would then give his leg the kind of burial given to a military hero. They wanted to hang the remainder of Arnold's body as a traitor. A monument on the battlefield at Saratoga shows Arnold's leg, but it does not mention him by name.

After the American Revolution ended in 1783, Arnold and his family divided their time between Canada and England. Arnold rebuilt his trading business. Arnold died in London on June 14, 1801.

Today, many Americans still call someone who commits treason a "Benedict Arnold."

GLOSSARY

brigadier (brig-uh-DEER)—the lowest of several levels within the military rank of general

civilian (si-VIL-yuhn)—a person who is not in the military

Continental Congress (KON-tuh-nen-tuhl KONG-griss)—leaders from the 13 original American Colonies that served as the American government from 1774 to 1789

court-martial (KORT-MAR-shuhl)—a military trial

loyalist (LOI-uh-list)—a colonist who was loyal to Great Britain during the Revolutionary War

patriot (PAY-tree-uht)—a person who sided with the colonies during the Revolutionary War

smuggle (SMUHG-uhl)—to sneak something in or out of a country illegally

treason (TREE-zuhn)—the act of turning against one's country

INTERNET SITES

FactHound offers a safe, fun way to find Internet sites related to this book. All of the sites on FactHound have been researched by our staff.

Here's how:
1. Visit *www.facthound.com*
2. Choose your grade level.
3. Type in this book ID **0736868542** for age-appropriate sites. You may also browse subjects by clicking on letters, or by clicking on pictures and words.
4. Click on the **Fetch It** button.

FactHound will fetch the best sites for you!

READ MORE

Anderson, Dale. *Leaders of the American Revolution.* World Almanac Library of the American Revolution. Milwaukee: World Almanac Library, 2006.

Bobrick, Benson. *Fight for Freedom: The American Revolutionary War.* New York: Atheneum Books for Young Readers, 2004.

Price Hossell, Karen. *Benedict Arnold.* American War Biographies. Chicago: Heinemann, 2004.

Sonneborn, Liz. *Benedict Arnold: Hero and Traitor.* Leaders of the American Revolution. Philadelphia: Chelsea House, 2006.

BIBLIOGRAPHY

Arnold, Isaac N. *The Life of Benedict Arnold: His Patriotism and His Treason.* Chicago: Jansen, McClurg and Company, 1880.

Brandt, Clare. *The Man in the Mirror: A Life of Benedict Arnold.* New York: Random House, 1994.

Fleming, Thomas. *Liberty! The American Revolution.* New York: Viking, 1997.

Randall, Willard Sterne. *Benedict Arnold: Patriot and Traitor.* New York: Morrow, 1990.

INDEX